★ ★

INDIANS OF AMERICA

Geronimo
APACHE WARRIOR

MATTHEW G. GRANT
Illustrated by John Keely and Dick Brude

GALLERY OF GREAT AMERICANS SERIES
★ ★

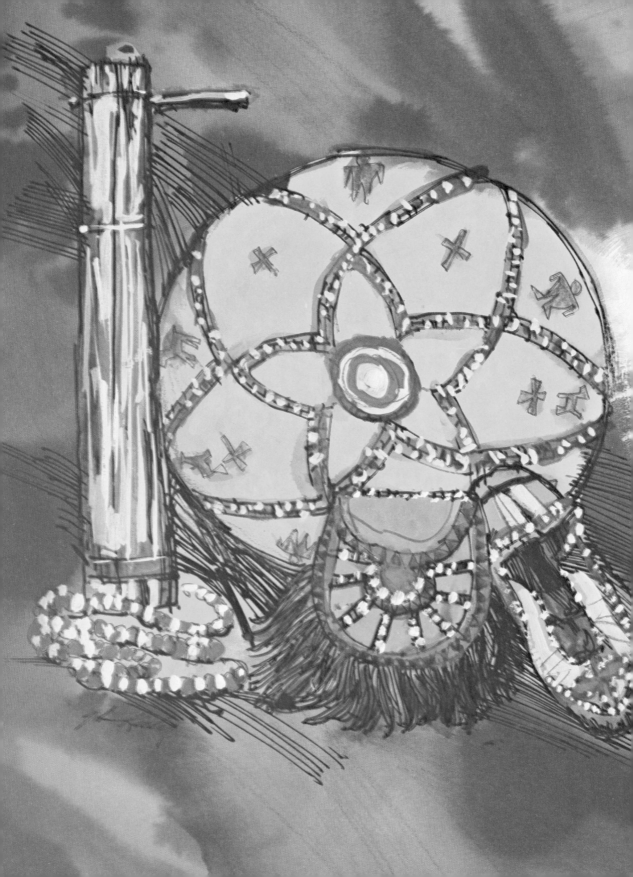

Geronimo
APACHE WARRIOR

Library of Congress Number: 73-12203

ISBN: 0-87191-267-8

Published by Creative Education, Mankato, Minnesota 56001

Library of Congress Cataloging in Publication Data
Grant, Matthew G
    Geronimo, Apache warrior.
    (His Indians of America) (Gallery of great Americans series)
    SUMMARY: A brief biography of the last of the Apache war chiefs to be subdued by the United States Army.
    1. Geronimo, Apache chief, 1829-1909—Juvenile literature. [1. Geronimo, Apache chief, 1829-1909. 2. Apache Indians—Biography. 3. Indians of North America—Biography] I. Keely, John, illus. II. Title. E99.A6G72 970.3 [B] [92] 73-12203
ISBN 0-87191-267-8

CONTENTS

AN APACHE BOY

A thousand years ago, a tribe of Indians left home. They moved from Canada to lands that are now part of New Mexico, Arizona, and Mexico. They were so fierce that other Indians called them apache, ''the enemy.''

7

There were many bands of Apaches. The Bedonkohe lived along the Gila River in Arizona. The men hunted deer, wild turkey, and sometimes buffalo. The women and children tended small gardens of corn, melons, and pumpkins. Most of the time, they were at peace.

In 1829 a boy named Goyakla — The Yawner — was born. His mother was the daughter of Chief Mahko. His father had come from the wild Nedni band, of Mexico.

Like most Apache children, Goyakla was not tall. But he was strong and brave, with a keen mind. His father trained him to run very fast, to ride a pony, and to hunt. He also helped his mother to farm.

All the time that Goyakla was small, he never saw a white man. But the Apaches in Mexico hated and feared the settlers. They raided the towns and ranches. The Mexican state of Sonora declared war.

Sonora said it would pay 100 pesos for each Apache warrior's scalp. A white trader in Arizona named James Johnson decided to make some money. He set up a trap for the friendly Bedonkohe Apaches that came to visit him. Using a cannon, he killed many — including the chief.

The new chief, Mangas Coloradas, said: "From now on, all white men are our enemies."

The talk of war was exciting to Goyakla. But he had to wait until he was 17 to become a warrior. By that time, most of the fighting seemed over. Mexico was going to sell the Arizona territory to the United States. The U.S. government wanted to make peace with the Apaches.

Goyakla married his childhood sweetheart, Alope. For three years, they and their people had peace.

THE NAMING OF GERONIMO

In 1851, the whole Bedonkohe band went south into Mexico to trade. But the Indians did not understand that the Mexicans were still at war with them. Mexican soldiers attacked the Apache camp near Janos.

Goyakla's mother, his young wife, and their three small children were all killed. So were many other members of the band. Chief Mangas Coloradas led his sorrowing people back to Arizona.

Goyakla had only one thought: revenge. The chief sent him to the Chiricahua Apache band to raise an army. Chief Cochise agreed

to join the fight against the Mexicans. The
Nedni Apaches joined them, too.

Goyakla was still a young man, but the chiefs of the three bands asked him to be their guide as they slipped into Mexico to take the warpath.

The Indians fought Mexican troops near Arizpe. Goyakla was their leader. In the terrible battle that followed, the Mexicans gave him a new name. They called him Geronimo. With enemy soldiers shouting his name, he led the Indians to victory.

THE APACHE WARS

In the years that followed, Goyakla became a famous raider, striking into Mexico from an Arizona base camp. Even the Indians began to call him Geronimo. He married a woman from Cochise's band.

The United States was supposed to be at peace with the Apaches. American settlers came into Arizona.

Geronimo was a member of Cochise's band, but he did not fight Americans — only Mexicans. For nearly ten years, the Chiricahua Apaches had peace.

Then, in 1861, a young army man accused Cochise of stealing cattle and kidnapping a white boy. He tried to arrest the chief. This started an Indian war.

Mangas Coloradas and his band joined with Cochise in fighting the U.S. Army. Geronimo was away, fighting in Mexico.

The Apaches attacked white settlements all over Arizona. In 1863 Mangas Coloradas was captured and killed by the Americans. Cochise became war chief of the entire tribe. Geronimo returned and fought with Cochise against the army for nearly ten years.

In 1871 the famous Indian fighter, General George Crook, was sent to put down the Apaches and make Arizona safe for white settlers. He was a wise man who determined to fight the Apaches in their own way. He enlisted Apaches as scouts in his army.

One by one, the Indian bands had to surrender. In 1872, even Cochise and Geronimo gave up and went to live on a reservation.

The proud Apaches were told to become farmers. Many refused. Geronimo finally led a group of these "renegade" Apaches into Mexico. Not long after, Cochise died. The only strong war leader left to the Apaches was Geronimo.

He and his warriors fought the whites in the best way they knew — killing, burning, and looting. They were only a few, but they were relentless.

Sometimes, when hardships overcame them, they would go back to the reservation for a short time. But then they would break out again. Year after year the raids went on. Once Geronimo was captured and imprisoned. But when he was set free, he went back to his old ways.

In 1885, General Crook received permission to pursue Geronimo into Mexico. His

army, facing terrible hardships, chased the Apaches into the wild Sierra Madre.

A WARRIOR'S END

The women and children in Geronimo's little band were suffering from the long pursuit. Most of the men now longed for peace. They were tired of hiding in the barren mountains.

Several times, General Crook offered to talk peace with Geronimo. Finally, in 1886, the Indian leader met with the American general. He agreed to surrender.

That night, a white trouble-maker brought liquor to the Apaches. Geronimo began to regret what he had done. Shots were fired by drunken Indians and Geronimo thought the band was being attacked. He and a few other Apaches fled into the mountains.

When the U.S. government learned Geronimo had escaped, General Crook was recalled. General Nelson A. Miles took up the pursuit of Geronimo. He chased the Apaches all summer. Finally his forces caught up with the old warrior and convinced him to surrender.

Geronimo said: "I will quit the warpath and live at peace hereafter." Then, surrounded by the U.S. Army, the Apaches marched north to Fort Bowie.

Geronimo and his people were imprisoned—first in Florida, then in Alabama. In 1892 they were sent to live at Fort Sill, Indian Territory. It was here that Geronimo died in 1909, still hoping that some day his people would be allowed to return to Arizona.

For a long time, white Americans believed Geronimo was an evil savage. Now he is known as a man of fierce courage who dared to fight for his land and people.

★ ★

GALLERY OF GREAT AMERICANS SERIES

★ ★

INDIANS OF AMERICA

- GERONIMO
- CRAZY HORSE
- CHIEF JOSEPH
- PONTIAC
- SQUANTO
- OSCEOLA

EXPLORERS OF AMERICA

- COLUMBUS
- LEIF ERICKSEN
- DeSOTO
- LEWIS AND CLARK
- CHAMPLAIN
- CORONADO

FRONTIERSMEN OF AMERICA

- DANIEL BOONE
- BUFFALO BILL
- JIM BRIDGER
- FRANCIS MARION
- DAVY CROCKET
- KIT CARSON

WAR HEROES OF AMERICA

- JOHN PAUL JONES
- PAUL REVERE
- ROBERT E. LEE
- ULYSSES S. GRANT
- SAM HOUSTON
- LAFAYETTE

WOMEN OF AMERICA

- CLARA BARTON
- JANE ADAMS
- ELIZABETH BLACKWELL
- HARRIET TUBMAN
- SUSAN B. ANTHONY
- DOLLY MADISON

★ ★